SIGHTSEERS
ESSENTIAL TRAVEL GUIDES TO THE PAST

ANCIENT
GREECE

A GUIDE TO THE GOLDEN
AGE OF GREECE

JULIE FERRIS

KINGFISHER

KINGFISHER
Kingfisher Publications Plc
New Penderel House,
283–288 High Holborn,
London WC1V 7HZ

Written and edited by Julie Ferris
Senior Designer Jane Tassie

Consultant David Nightingale
Illustrations Inklink Firenze
Kevin Maddison

Editorial assistance Katie Puckett
Research Prue Grice
DTP Co-ordinator Nicky Studdart
Production Controller Kelly Johnson
Picture Research Manager Jane Lambert
Proofreader Sheila Clewley
Indexer Sylvia Potter

First published by Kingfisher Publications Plc 1999
3 5 7 9 10 8 6 4 2

2TR/0799/WKT/UNV(UNV)/140MA

A CIP catalogue record for this book is available from the
British Library.

ISBN 0 7534 0374 9

Printed in
Hong Kong/China

Contents

Introducing Greece

There has never been a better time to visit Ancient Greece. Made up of small, independent city-states around the Mediterranean coast, Greece is currently experiencing a cultural golden age. The relative peace between the often warring cities has allowed the arts, theatre, politics, philosophy and science to flourish.

Athens is a democracy and one if its most influential statesmen is Pericles. He is usually portrayed wearing a helmet and is rumoured to have a slightly misshapen head.

Sightseers' tip
The city-state of Athens would make a good base for your holiday. It has an impressive political system, and the recently built Parthenon temple on the Acropolis is well worth a visit.

Over 800 years before the Golden Age, Mycenaeans lived in Greece. They were famed for their gold treasures.

Greeks began to venture out from their homeland and to establish colonies around the coasts of the Mediterranean.

The first Olympic Games were held 270 years before the Golden Age. Around the same time, writing was developed.

 For most of the year Greece is mild, but in summer it is very hot and dusty.

 A city-state comprises the city itself and the countryside surrounding it.

Female travellers beware – women are rarely allowed out of the home.

Dominating the Athens skyline is the Acropolis. Once a hilltop fort, it is now a holy place with stunning temples. Athens is the largest and most powerful of the Greek city-states and has a population of about 250,000.

Athens is ruled by democracy, which means that all male citizens can take part in the government of the city. This freedom of speech means that relations between the rich and poor are considerably better than in other city-states. Citizens have a say in the running of the city and therefore do not resent the wealthy landowners. However, some aristocrats complain that they are not given enough respect, and that the poor don't move out of their way in the streets! Other city-states, such as Sparta, are ruled by kings or small groups of aristocrats.

A system of democracy evolved in Athens. All male citizens are given a say in how the state is governed.

For ten years before the Golden Age began, Greece was locked in war with Persia, a middle eastern empire.

Athens' victory in the Persian Wars reinvigorates Greek culture, and the Acropolis is rebuilt.

Travelling about

The Greeks are considered great sailors, and if you attempt to cross the mountainous inland regions you will discover why. To avoid a long, steep trek by donkey, board one of the many ships that arrive and depart from Athens' famous harbour, Piraeus.

If you want to travel inland, hire a donkey to make the journey less tiring. Make sure you wear a wide-brimmed straw hat to protect you from the hot sun.

Big eyes are painted on the sides of the prow of Greek ships to scare away evil spirits and protect the sailors.

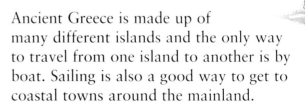

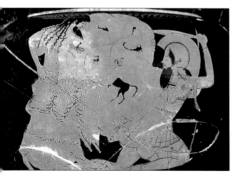

Ancient Greece is made up of many different islands and the only way to travel from one island to another is by boat. Sailing is also a good way to get to coastal towns around the mainland.

Poseidon, the god of the sea, carries a trident – a spear with three prongs. Greeks believe he has the power to prevent shipwrecks and make offerings of wine to him.

Piraeus harbour is 6 km from Athens and is connected to the city by a walled corridor.

Avoid travelling on merchant ships. They are slow and easily captured by pirates.

Greek sailors like to keep sight of the coast and will not sail in bad weather.

Avoid visiting Greece during the winter months when travel practically comes to a halt. Winters tend to be very wet, making mountain tracks impassable. Sailing also becomes difficult because boat sails get wet and visibility is poor.

Sightseers' tip
Along the rough, stony roads inland are inns and shops for travellers. However, their reputation is not good. Comedy writers often include jokes about cheating innkeepers in their plays!

What to wear

To look the part in Athens you can't go wrong with a simple chiton (pronounced "kye-ton"). Made from linen or wool, the chiton is little more than a tube of material pinned or sewn over the shoulders. Over the chiton Greeks drape a hard-wearing woollen cloak called a himation.

To take a shower, Greeks sit in a large pottery bowl while a slave pours cool water over them.

Sightseers' tip

It is a sign of good breeding and elegance to have your himation arranged correctly. If it is too short, your neighbours will laugh at you, too long and it will drag in the mud. Himations are expensive to make and are a popular target for thieves.

You can buy clothes in the market, but they are expensive!

 Look out for girls wearing high-heeled sandals to make them taller.

 Greeks don't wear underwear. If you are cold put on another chiton.

Women wear their chitons to the ankle and dye them bright colours such as red, yellow, green and purple.

Greek women are rarely allowed to leave the house. When they do they wear their finest jewellery. Hairpins, rings and earrings can be purchased from travelling pedlars.

Make sure you visit a barber shop while in Athens. It is a popular place to meet and exchange news and gossip. Greek men tend to keep their hair short and most have beards. Women tie their long hair up in carefully arranged styles. Blonde hair is greatly admired and many women have tried using bleach.

Although Greeks go barefoot in the home, comfy leather sandals are worn in the street. You can have them custom made by a cobbler. He will ask you to stand on the leather while he draws around your foot.

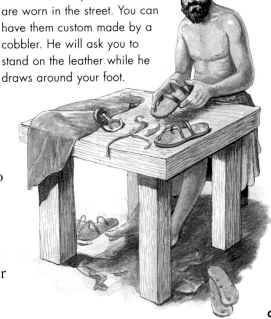

It is very fashionable for women to have pale skin. Poor women have suntans from working outside and often paint their faces with white lead to look paler. Be warned! The lead can bring you out in a rash, or even kill you if you use too much.

Food and drink

Unless you are dining with aristocrats, food in Ancient Greece tends to be quite basic and the meals informal. Meat is very expensive and the poor only eat it at religious festivals.

Sightseers' tip Professional cooks are hired for symposions. Slaves are sent out with invitations – small statues showing people eating or walking to a feast.

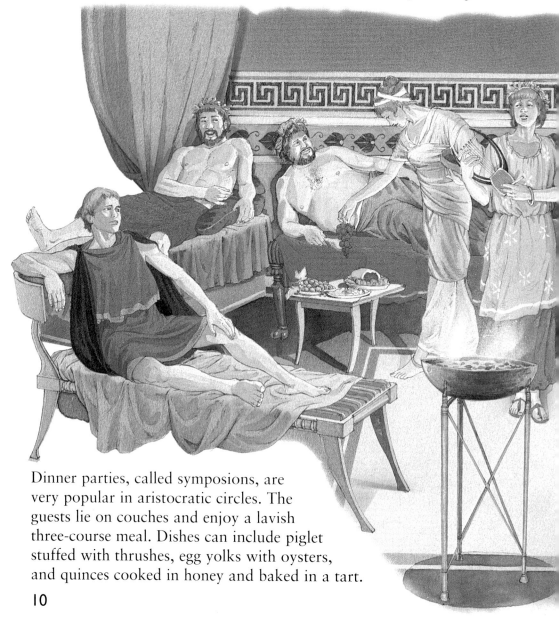

Dinner parties, called symposions, are very popular in aristocratic circles. The guests lie on couches and enjoy a lavish three-course meal. Dishes can include piglet stuffed with thrushes, egg yolks with oysters, and quinces cooked in honey and baked in a tart.

Greeks eat meals outdoors during the day. Evening meals are eaten at sunset.

Animals are sacrificed at religious festivals and offerings of food and wine are made.

Peasants drink goat's milk or water. Wine is often diluted.

Wine is drunk from a broad, shallow cup called a kylix. Drinking games are popular at symposions.

Women prepare all the food. Cooking is done over a charcoal fire and bronze or clay utensils are used.

Slaves at the symposion dinner will cut up your food for you, and sometimes even feed you. After the meal, acrobats, dancing girls and musicians perform for the guests and vast quantities of wine are drunk. Stories and jokes are told, and very often politics is discussed. Female visitors, however, are unlikely to be invited to a symposion. The only women allowed to attend are slaves and entertainers.

Bread, gruel, olives, figs and cheese made from goat's milk are the most common foods. Cheap, fresh fish is available in coastal towns.

Shopping

The best place for shopping in Athens, as in any Greek city-state, is the agora, or market-place. Everything from meat, fish, vegetables and fruit, to pottery, bronze ware and textiles is available from the market stalls and shops. You will even be able to buy slaves! The agora is the centre of Athenian life and men spend most of their day there.

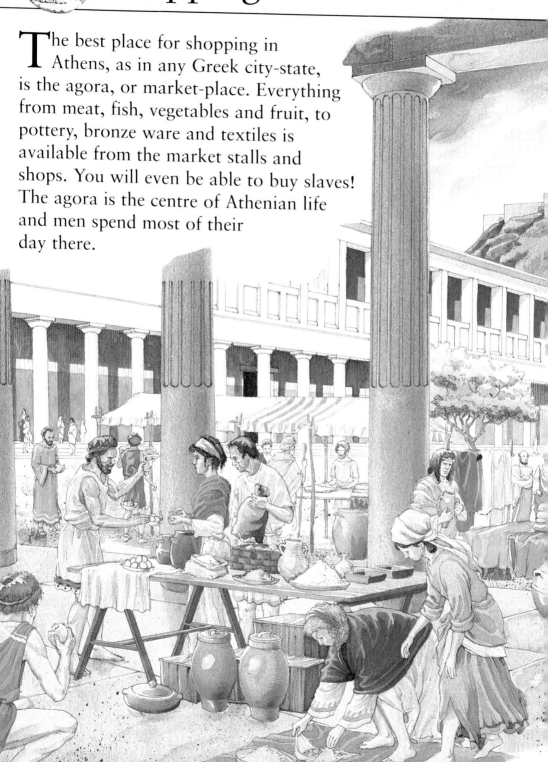

Why not commission a sculptor to make you a statue of a god to bring you luck?

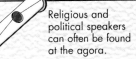

There are no pockets in Greek clothing – it is customary to carry coins in your mouth.

Religious and political speakers can often be found at the agora.

Sightseers' tip ✔

At the agora you will find finely carved marble figures and bronze statues. Pottery bowls, vases and cups decorated with scenes of Greek life and paintings of gods and heroes are also available.

The most common Athenian coin has a picture of Athena, goddess of the city, on one side. On the other side is her emblem, an owl.

If it gets too hot in the middle of the day, why not take a stroll round the stoa, the sheltered colonnade on the edges of the agora? Shoemakers, ironmongers, carpenters, money-lenders and doctors are all to be found in the stoa, as well as the offices of lawyers and magistrates.

In the stoa you may well see a philosopher explaining his ideas, or a storyteller recounting tales of the gods and heroes. The most famous stories, the *Iliad* and the *Odyssey*, describe the war between Greece and Troy.

13

Accommodation

To fully experience Ancient Greece, stay as a guest in a typical Greek house. They are made of mud bricks and have tiled roofs. The rooms are all on one floor and are built around an open-air courtyard where women relax and chat to one another, the family eats its meals, and children play.

Sightseers' tip Keep your valuables safe! The mud bricks are quite soft and it is easy for burglars to cut through the walls!

Most Greek households have slaves. Male slaves guard the house and do the shopping. Female slaves do the cooking and cleaning.

Three-legged furniture is very common. It can stand on any surface, even bumpy earth floors.

As wood is scarce in mountainous Greece, most houses are poorly furnished.

 Many houses contain a small shrine in the courtyard where you can worship the gods.

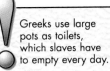 Greeks use large pots as toilets, which slaves have to empty every day.

Clay oil lamps are lit at night. Oil is poured in the middle and a wick is placed in the spout.

Greek women are only allowed to leave their homes for short periods of time. They are not even supposed to open the outer door of the house in case they come face to face with a man. While boys are at school, girls learn to run the house by helping their mothers.

15

The theatre

No trip to Ancient Greece would be complete without a visit to the theatre. The semicircular theatre in Athens can hold over 10,000 people and entry costs two obols. Performances are held once a month, and last all day. However, make sure you get there early – the theatre is usually full by dawn! If you enjoy serious drama, you could watch a Greek tragedy. If you prefer boisterous, and often vulgar, entertainment, go and see a comedy.

If you get bored between plays, make use of one of the game boards scratched on some of the seats.

Sightseers' tip Show your appreciation by whistling and stamping your feet. Don't get too rowdy – theatre staff may beat you with a stick!

Bring plenty to eat and drink as the performances last all day.

 Drama was invented in Athens as part of the spring festival for the god Dionysus.

 Look out for the important officials who sit in ceremonial seats at the front.

No more than three actors in each play take the various speaking roles, changing masks to show which character they are playing. A chorus of around 15 actors sings or chants parts of the story. Although women are allowed to go to the theatre, all roles in the plays, including female ones, are played by men.

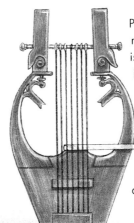

Plays often include music. The lyre, which is similar to a harp, is the most popular instrument. You will also see musicians playing the double flute. It is difficult to play as it requires twice as much breath as a single flute.

The assembly

Athens is a democracy, and every Athenian citizen has a say in the running of the city. Important matters are debated and decided at the assembly. This is held, on average, every nine days on the slopes of the Pynx Hill. There have to be at least 6,000 citizens at each assembly.

To prevent anyone speaking for too long during a debate, speeches are timed with a water clock.

Sightseers' tip   Make sure you arrive in good time. Those who are slow to enter the assembly are forced to hurry. A rope dipped in red paint herds people in. If you dawdle you will get paint on your clothes and have to pay a fine.

Women and slaves are not allowed to speak or vote at an assembly.

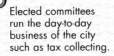
Elected committees run the day-to-day business of the city such as tax collecting.

Speeches can be very entertaining and speakers often taunt each other.

Although anyone is allowed to stand up and make a speech, it is so daunting that usually only the well-educated dare to do it. Rival speakers jeer at each other and try to persuade the crowd that their ideas are the best. Slave archers keep order in case a discussion becomes rowdy. When a matter has been fully debated, citizens vote by raising their hands.

Juries vote by dropping bronze ballots with hollow (guilty) or solid (innocent) shafts into a box. By holding the ballot between finger and thumb, you can stop people seeing which way you vote.

The atmosphere at trials in Athens is often tense and the trials are usually rowdy as jurors are allowed to shout questions at the defendants or prosecutors. The juries are very large – sometimes thousands in important cases. This makes them difficult to bribe. After all the evidence has been heard, the jurors vote for whoever they feel has presented the most convincing argument.

The Acropolis

One of the most picturesque attractions that Athens has to offer is the Acropolis, or "highest city". Built originally as a fortress, the Acropolis has recently been redeveloped. At its centre is a splendid new temple called the Parthenon.

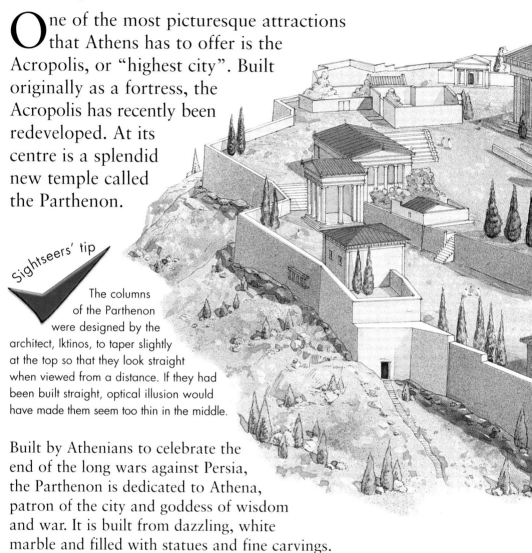

Sightseers' tip

The columns of the Parthenon were designed by the architect, Iktinos, to taper slightly at the top so that they look straight when viewed from a distance. If they had been built straight, optical illusion would have made them seem too thin in the middle.

Built by Athenians to celebrate the end of the long wars against Persia, the Parthenon is dedicated to Athena, patron of the city and goddess of wisdom and war. It is built from dazzling, white marble and filled with statues and fine carvings.

There is a large family of gods, each with different powers. Apollo is god of the arts, Aphrodite is goddess of love and Zeus is king of all the gods.

If you can't afford to give an animal sacrifice at the temple, offer a pastry sacrifice instead.

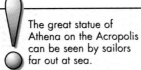 The great statue of Athena on the Acropolis can be seen by sailors far out at sea.

 Athena is believed to have been born fully formed from Zeus's forehead.

Friezes in the Parthenon commemorate the Panathenaia festival, held every July in honour of Athena. There is singing, dancing, athletics and a temple procession.

There are no weekends in Ancient Greece, so people look forward particularly to the 40 religious festivals held each year in Athens. As well as time off work, there is always a lot of free food, drink and entertainment on offer during festivals.

Look out for one of these coin-operated water dispensers when you visit the Parthenon temple.

The Olympic Games

The gods are believed to live in the clouds above Mount Olympus. Although named after the mountain, Olympia is a long way from it.

Try to time your visit to Ancient Greece to coincide with the Olympic Games in Olympia. They are held every four years in honour of Zeus, king of the gods, and are open to athletes from all over Greece. Events include running, chariot racing, long jump, javelin, discus and fighting.

There is a luxury hotel for officials, but most visitors sleep in the open.

 The Games are held every four years in July, and admission is free.

 Make sure you see the massive gold and ivory statue of Zeus at Olympia.

The fiercest event at the Games is the pankration, a cross between boxing and wrestling. Only eye-gouging and biting are against the rules.

The Games are taken very seriously. Even in times of war a truce is declared so that the Games can go ahead.

Sightseers' tip

Because the athletes compete naked, women are not allowed to watch under any circumstance. However, they hold their own games in honour of the goddess Hera, wife of Zeus.

The stadium has room for about 40,000 spectators. Only the judges have seats, so you will have to stand or sit on the surrounding hillside. Dancers and jugglers entertain the crowds in between events, and there are food stalls for refreshments. Remember, wearing a hat is forbidden in case it blocks someone's view.

Winners are presented with a wreath of olive leaves cut from a sacred tree.

23

Sparta

The city-state of Sparta in southern Greece is a fascinating place to visit. In contrast to the rest of Greece, Sparta's entire culture is based on maintaining its full-time army. Citizens are forbidden to work and there are no holidays. Life in Sparta is an endless cycle of military drills and exercises.

Bravery is very important to the Spartans. You will have no problem identifying a coward. Half his hair and half his beard is shaved off and he is jeered at in the street.

Spartan citizens have to do 23 years' compulsory military training. Land slaves called helots work the fields and feed the Spartans. The helots are treated very cruelly.

You may not want to stay long – by Athenian standards, life in Sparta is very tough and dull.

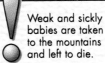
Weak and sickly babies are taken to the mountains and left to die.

Spartans eat a black broth made of pork, stock, vinegar and salt.

One of the first things you'll see when you arrive in Sparta is a group of men or boys training for war. Spartans have little family life. They believe that warriors should be loyal to their community and not to their relations. Boys are sent to military school at the age of seven, and they live and train in the barracks until their military service ends.

Women in Sparta are expected to exercise and keep fit so that they will produce strong, healthy babies.

Spartans learn to move stealthily in the dark, to steal food and to live with few clothes or possessions. They are not encouraged to read books for fear that they will develop their own ideas.

Sightseers' tip

Spartan soldiers are very organized and disciplined. You may see Spartan men marching in a formation called a phalanx – side by side in tight rows.

25

The countryside

Most Athenians own small-holdings in the country. Even though there is not much fertile soil, the Greeks make the most of the land and grow fig trees, vines, olive trees, wheat and barley. The land owner and his slaves do all the work by hand.

Fishing is very important in Greece. Trawling nets are used out at sea, and fishing rods are used in rivers and lakes.

Sightseers' tip

Rather than pick olives one by one from a tree, farmers beat the branches with a stick to make the ripe fruit fall to the floor. Then the olives are put in a press and the oil is squeezed from them.

Olive oil is sometimes presented as a prize to athletes at the Olympic Games.

 A lot of food is imported into Greece. Eels from Boeotia are a favourite in Athens.

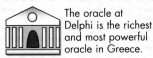 The oracle at Delphi is the richest and most powerful oracle in Greece.

The priestess at Delphi speaks to the gods when she is in a trance. The gods communicate with her in riddles which are translated by the priests.

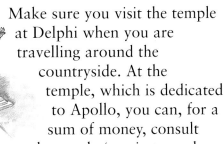

Make sure you visit the temple at Delphi when you are travelling around the countryside. At the temple, which is dedicated to Apollo, you can, for a sum of money, consult the oracle (a priestess who speaks to the gods on your behalf) and discover what the future holds for you. Greek cities often consult the oracle at Delphi for political advice.

Survival guide

Visitors to Ancient Greece may find it difficult to travel around. Not only is there much rivalry between the different city-states, there is also a general dislike of foreigners as Greeks consider themselves to be culturally superior. Take care – many outsiders end up as slaves!

Health

Health care in Ancient Greece is very sophisticated. If you have cause to visit a doctor you will be asked what your symptoms are, what sort of food you eat and whether you take exercise. Once the doctor has all relevant information written down, he will prescribe a herbal cure. Health is considered the greatest gift of the gods to man.

Greek doctors are generally well-dressed, cheerful and highly knowledgeable. One doctor, Hippocrates of Cos, has written down the methods a doctor must follow.

Administration

Most Greek boys learn how to read and write. Ink is made from soot or taken from cuttlefish, and bark or papyrus are commonly used as paper. Many walls have carved inscriptions.

The main units of money are the obol and the drachma (worth about six obols). Visitors will soon be familiar with half-obol, obol, drachma and two- and four-drachma coins. Citizens in Athens earn about half a drachma a day. Units of length are the finger (19.3 mm) and the foot. There are 16 fingers to the foot.

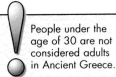
People under the age of 30 are not considered adults in Ancient Greece.

Slaves are not allowed to use their own names – their owners have the right to rename them.

Unusually, in Athens the police force is made up of slaves.

If you are planning a long visit to Athens, make sure you do not become too powerful or you could face ostracism – banishment from the state for a period of ten years.

Citizens bring to the meeting small pieces of broken pottery called ostraka. On each ostrakon is scratched the name of the person the citizen wants to ostracize.

Every year a meeting is held and citizens are invited to write down the name of the person they most want to get rid of. If enough people write the same man's name, he will be ostracized.

29

❓Souvenir quiz

Take your time exploring Ancient Greece. It is a fascinating land with plenty to see and experience. Before you leave, test your knowledge with this fun quiz. You will find the answers on page 32.

1. Why do Greeks usually travel by boat rather than going overland?

a) Because there are bandits and thieves lurking on many of the inland roads ready to attack unsuspecting travellers.

b) Because the inland regions are very mountainous and difficult to cross.

c) Because Greeks do not want to upset Poseidon, god of the sea.

2. Why is pale skin considered the height of fashion for Greek women?

a) It shows that they come from such a wealthy and respectable family that they do not need to work outside in the sun.

b) They are worried about the harmful effects of the sun on their skin.

c) Pale skin complements their brightly coloured chitons.

3. Why does Greek furniture often have only three legs?

a) Three-legged furniture can stand more firmly on bumpy earth floors.

b) Wood is scarce in Greece and it is too expensive to make furniture with four legs.

c) The number three has religious importance.

4. How do Greeks show their appreciation at the theatre?

a) By clapping their hands.

b) By shouting at the actors.

c) By whistling and stamping their feet.

5. Who is allowed to speak at an assembly?

a) Anyone in Greece.

b) Any citizen of the city-state of Athens.

c) Aristocrats and important citizens.

6. Spartan men have to do 23 years' military training. Why are Spartan women expected to exercise and keep fit?

a) So that they produce strong, healthy babies.

b) So that they will be ready to fight and defend Sparta against attack.

c) So that they are strong enough to stop the helots (the land slaves that work the fields and cook the food) from rebelling.

7. An assembly is called in Athens roughly every nine days. Who keeps order at the assembly?

a) Officials elected by the assembly each year.

b) The oldest citizens at the assembly.

c) Slave archers wearing special caps and capes.

8. Greeks believe there is a family of gods. Where are the gods believed to live?

a) In the clouds above Mount Olympus.

b) In the Parthenon temple on the Acropolis.

c) In the sea.

9. The Olympic Games are held in Olympia every four years. What prize is presented to the triumphant winners at the Games?

a) A large sum of money.

b) A wreath of olive leaves cut from a sacred tree.

c) A medal made of gold.

10. To find out what the future has in store, Greeks travel to Delphi and consult the oracle. What is the oracle?

a) An ancient prophecy inscribed on tablets of stone.

b) A statue of the god Apollo.

c) A priestess who has the power to speak to the gods.

31

Index

Acknowledgements

Design assistance
Joanne Brown

The consultant
David Nightingale M.A. (Oxon) teaches Greek and Roman history at the University of Kent at Canterbury. He is a regular visitor to Athens and Greece.

Inklink Firenze illustrators
Simone Boni, Alessandro Rabatti, Lorenzo Pieri, Luigi Critone, Lucia Mattioli, Francisco Petracchi, Theo Caneschi.

Additional illustrations
Vanessa Card, Terry Gabbey, Ian Jackson, Nicki Palin, David Salariya/Shirley Willis, Thomas Trojer.

Picture credits
b = bottom, c = centre, l = left, r = right, t = top
p.4c British Museum/Michael Holford; p.6bl Vienna Kunsthistorisches Museum/AKG London; p.9tr British Museum/Michael Holford; p.11tr Ancient Art and Architecture, tl Corbis UK/Araldo de Luca; p.13c AKG London; p.15cr British Museum; p.16tr Ancient Art & Architecture; p. 19cr American School of Classical Studies, Athens; p.21tr British Museum/Michael Holford; p.22tl Corbis UK/Robert Gill; p.23tl British Museum/Michael Holford; p.25tr British Museum/Michael Holford; p.26tl Erich Lessing/ AKG London; p.28cr British Museum/Michael Holford; p. 29tr Corbis UK/Gianni Dagli Orti.

Every effort has been made to trace the copyright holders of the photographs. The publishers apologise for any inconvenience caused.

Souvenir quiz answers

1 = b) 2 = a) 3 = a) 4 = c) 5 = b) 6 = a) 7 = c) 8 = a) 9 = b) 10 = c)   *This book is set in 432 BC.*